Jean Charlier de Gerson

The snares of the devil

Jean Charlier de Gerson

The snares of the devil

ISBN/EAN: 9783741194863

Manufactured in Europe, USA, Canada, Australia, Japa

Cover: Foto ©Andreas Hilbeck / pixelio.de

Manufactured and distributed by brebook publishing software (www.brebook.com)

Jean Charlier de Gerson

The snares of the devil

THE
Snares of the Devil.

BY

JOHN GERSON,

CHANCELLOR OF PARIS,

Surnamed the Most Christian Doctor.

TRANSLATED BY BETA.

London:
THOMAS RICHARDSON AND SON,
28, KING EDWARD STREET, CITY;
AND DERBY.
1883.

Biographical Notice.

John Charlier Gerson, a celebrated French theologian, surnamed the Mòst Christian Doctor, was born on the 14th of December, 1363, at Gerson, a hamlet in the diocese in Rheims, near to Rethel. He died at Lyons, in a Monastery of Celestine Monks, on the 12th of July, 1429. He was the eldest of twelve children. His parents, Arnulph Charlier and Elizabeth Lachardeniere, brought up their family in a religious manner. Gerson himself tells us that three of his brothers and four sisters embraced the yoke of Christ in the conventual life. It was beneath the shadow of the Cloister that peace-loving souls, or those wounded in the struggle of life, sought for rest and shelter, away from the tumult of a corrupt and wicked age.

Gerson spent his early youth at home. If credence is to be given to d'Arquetil, he began his studies at Rheims, and there he acquired his classical taste, especially for poetry, which ever after distinguished him. At fourteen he was sent to Paris, and in 1377 he was placed on the foundation in the College of Navarre. Here, according to the frequent usage of the time, he changed his family name for that of the hamlet where he was born. This renouncing of the paternal name symbolised death to self and to one's own family. By thus loosening the ties of kindred, the chains which fettered man to his own narrow interests and passions were broken in sunder, and a sort of impersonality was accepted.

The following year was darkened by the cloud of the great Schism of the West, which passed over Christendom. Urban VI. was elected in Rome, April 1378, and Clement VII. in Avignon in the September of the same year. From this time there began, for the Christian world, for Holy Church, and for the Papacy, one of those fearful epochs, full of present misery, and pregnant with sorrow for the future. Then was it needful that some brave and mighty spirit should come forward, to undertake the task of restoring peace to the conscience, union and purity to the Church, and of rehabilitating the Holy See in her former greatness. Such was the work to which Gerson consecrated all the power of his intellect and the strength of his will; though in truth he seemed more fitted for the tranquillity of the Cloister, and for contemplation, than for the harassing tumult of an active public life.

While he was earnestly imploring help from God to heal the wounds of His Church, he raised his voice in expostulation against the foolish subtleties in which thinking minds were then losing themselves.

"It is needful," he said, "to sweep away these cobwebs, whose threads, too closely woven, break one another in their interlace....... The teaching of wisdom should be solid, it should shine forth more by clearness than astonish by its over-nicety. A fine thing it is indeed, to transcribe Homer's Illiad in microscopic letters, so as to fit the whole in a nutshell! Man should strive to make himself useful, and not be ever seeking to excite admiration."

Thus, before receiving the title of Chancellor, which

gave him authority to reform philosophical studies, he endeavoured to lead to clearer and more practical wisdom those minds which were then drifting down the stream of vain and futile thought.

In 1392 Gerson had received the doctor's cap from the hands of his former master, d'Ailly.

Three years before, d'Ailly, who had been successively promoted to the Bishoprics of Puy (1395), and of Cambray (1396), had chosen Gerson as his successor to the office of Chancellor to the University, and to the Church of Notre Dame de Paris. This choice had been seconded by the Duke of Burgundy, whose almoner Gerson was. With the honour of Chancellor fresh duties fell to the lot of Gerson, and the weight of the renewed burden affrighted him. Envious tongues made his fair name their plaything, and wicked men, whose passions Gerson had condemned, darkened it by their odious calumnies. Sick in body, troubled in mind, and fearful for the future, he thought of withdrawing to Bruges, there to fulfil, in greater tranquillity, the duties of Capitular of the Cathedral of S. Donatas, which office Philip the Hardy had conferred on him. The benefice was, however, disputed, and this led Gerson to go to Bruges to uphold his rights. He tarried in the old Flemish town for some time, often preaching to the people.

Nothing but the earnest entreaties of his friends, and, in particular, those of his patron, the Duke of Burgundy, could determine Gerson to bear the heavy responsibility of the Chancellor's office. From the moment, however, of its acceptance, he generously made the sacrifice of his love of solitude and of peace. From that time the words of the Imitation seemed to have been his motto: "Strive manfully." The longing for the end of the strife, mingled with so much bitter sorrow, was shown in the words which escaped from his heart in a sermon which Gerson preached at Tarascon, in presence of Benedict, "Peace, peace, oh that peace may descend; above all things I long and yearn for peace."

The Chancellor's first struggle was on the field of science, against the schoolmen. In two letters, written from Bruges to the students of the college of Navarre, he complains of their restless and tumultuous spirit, of their foolish disputes about trifles, and of weakening the thoughts of the great doctors by too great a subtlety in their arguments and reasoning. He also gives advice on the choice of books. "There are some authors," he writes, "whom it is only needful to salute in passing, as a sign that we are not ignorant of them. A few, such as S. Bonaventure, S. Thomas, and William of Auxerre, should be known to us as intimate friends. As to pagan writers, we must in no wise give ourselves up to them, but be contented to be their passing guest."

In another work the reform which Gerson sought to make in the students' studies, especially in theology, is marked by a still greater precision. The criticisms which he passed on scholastic philosophy display a mind at once elevated and firm.

In 1414 was convoked the Council of Constance; it lasted until 1418, at which Gregory XII. voluntarily resigned. The anti-Popes, John XXII. and Benedict XIII. were deposed, and a new Pope was elected, who took the name of Martin V., and thus the great Schism of the West was healed.

John Gerson.

Gerson assisted at the Council as Ambassador of the French King. While he was away on this mission Paris was the scene of civil discord, and on the termination of the Council he was unable to return thither. In pilgrim's garb he wandered amid the mountains of Bavaria, and in the Tyrol, passing from thence to Vienna, where Duke Frederick of Austria made him welcome, and named him professor of the University. He remained here for some months, but in 1419 the murder of the Duke of Burgundy enabled him to return to France. He went to Lyons, where the party for the Dauphin predominated. John, Prior of a Convent of Celestine Monks, offered him a home, which he accepted. This John de Gerson is called his brother (germanus), but it is unlikely that two brothers were both named John. Germanus means only near kinsman. He was probably his cousin. The declining years of the great Chancellor passed peacefully in the exercise of prayer and contemplation, beneath the shade of the Monastery of the Church of S. Paul. He now blessed the trials through which he had passed, and which had led him to his peaceful retreat in the evening of life. He did not, however, withdraw into selfish solitude, he still yearned for the welfare of the souls of men; he frequently gave instructions, and he was at once edifying by his words and work. He encouraged and advised all those who sought his counsel. It was during his sojourn in Lyons that Gerson wrote almost all his works on mystic philosophy, his Commentaries on the Psalms, and his treatise on the Examination of Doctrine. It is said that he took especial delight in little children; it was, he said, through them that the reformation of the Church must be begun. He loved to gather the children of the poor around him, and to teach them the catechism. It was a touching sight to see this venerable man, whose words had thrilled the Christian world, surrounded by God's little ones, explaining the deep mysteries of faith to them, or teaching them the rudiments of the Latin tongue. "O God, my Creator! have pity on Thy servant, John Gerson," was the simple prayer he taught their infant lips to say for him.

Gerson's last work was a Commentary on the Canticles; it was finished just before his death, which occurred on the 12th of July, 1429, when he was in his 67th year. His body was buried in the Church of S. Paul. On his tomb were inscribed the words which mark so well his own inner life: "Sursum corda." For a long time his resting-place was held sacred; the people of Lyons flocked to pray there, and it is said that miracles were not wanting to testify to his great holiness.

PREFACE OF THE AUTHOR.

It has been proposed to me to unfold some of those crafty wiles by which the enemy of the human race lays snares for us in all our works. We may thus learn to humble ourselves under the hand of God; we may procure, at least in a general manner, a knowledge of how ignorant we are in the path of virtue, and we may get to see how helplessly weak we are against all the wicked malice of this foe, unless we put our trust in the assistance of God and of His Saints. For the devil insinuates himself, by deceptive ambushes, into all our thoughts, words, and works. He especially thus attacks those whom he perceives to be very earnestly intent on serving God faithfully;

and if he can he will turn them to evil, under the specious guise of good.

Like a deceitful robber, when he falls in with the good he offers himself as a companion of the journey, and converses with them. And till a fair opportunity comes of striking and killing the soul, he feigns a most trusty friendship. But when he has bided his time, he strives to defile some holy action by cunningly mingling with it the poison of his malice, so to ruin it, either in the beginning, the middle, or the end.

When the devil cannot prevent a good action, he strives to spoil the intention and make it corrupt, as, e.g., to do the good thing for vain-glory, or some carnal pleasure. If, however, the beginning of the action has eluded his grasp, he then tries to seize it in the middle, or at least in the finish; and even after its completion he still loiters about, for he may yet contrive to move a man to a vain gladness at having well performed a virtuous work.

Supposing a man wants to give an alms: when the enemy cannot hinder him, he exhorts him to obtain some worldly praise by it, or to have in view some equivalent advantage from him to whom it is given, some gift, or some service. And if this temptation is overcome, he prepares another more subtle and efficacious, so common to the good, that in this life it is scarce possible, I fancy, to be without; and it is this—he incites a man to think and say with himself: "There, you have done your work well; you have managed well to defeat the enemy; no vain-glory or other vice has been mixed with your good action. Another—this one or that—would not have so done." So he who had overcome vain-glory before, and pride, now falls headlong to his ruin by the same vices. Yet such rash and silly thoughts almost always insinuate themselves into the mind. It is plain then, that unless we take great care, our virtue may become a vice, and pride may spring even from humility.

Snares of the Devil.

CHAPTER I.

Of Vice under the semblance of Virtue.

The devil sometimes advises us to put aside all striving after very lofty virtue, and to occupy ourselves instead in things of little moment. He does this, either to take us altogether out of the road of any great perfection, or that by this sort of bastard humility we may fancy we have an extraordinary sanctity in avoiding a lofty state, and not seeking high things. By this a secret pride may be engendered in the soul, and a rash judging of others, who do not walk in the same path.

2. Sometimes the enemy counsels to say an immense multitude of prayers out of custom. His object in this is to render the task burdensome and tiresome, so that they shall be void of devotion, and without unction; or again that, by considering the number of prayers said, the person may be lifted up with pride. Sometimes, too, he does it to hinder the person from works which would be more profitable, or which are more necessary. Or again, he thus tempts the soul to fancy that by the frequency of her prayers she can oblige God by right to accomplish what she covets.

3. Frequently the devil hinders people from doing good things from a fear lest they should be called Saints, or should be thought Saints, and so should become proud. So he causes a person to imagine

that spiritual sloth is a discreet humility. He will not allow the withholding of alms to be called avarice, nor the giving up fasting to be gluttony, but he terms it a high and excellent virtue of humility.

4. Under guise of giving correction the devil incites some either to anger or to a put on anger. He does this that a person may go further than he ought in correction, using injurious or insulting expressions; or perhaps from anger, seeking rather the indulgence of a spiteful malice than the culprit's good. The devil often has another object to gain, for by the rude harshness of the correction, the person found fault with, instead of mending, becomes far worse than before. For to gain a person to good an exceeding rigour is not near so efficacious as a gentle, mild way. In like manner, impatience, injustice, revengefulness, &c., are covered

under the veil of correction; and such correction is not really correction at all, but destruction.

5. Sometimes the devil, under pretext of a wise discretion, advises more sleep and food, so as under colour of prudence to introduce into the soul the vices of gluttony and sloth; forbidding fasts and abstinence.

6. Heady and unruly persons the devil pushes sometimes to seek frequent counsel of the wise, knowing well that they will not follow the advice they receive, and so will sin on with less excuse than before. Sometimes he gets foolish persons to confide blindly in foolish advisers, so that the one who gives the advice, and the one who follows it, may both perish together.

7. Sometimes the devil depreciates all counsel of man, and exhorts the soul to look to God alone, and to expect from Him instruction in prayer. Or he tells a man it is

safest to rely on his own judgment. For, says he, in this thing that you think to do, who knows better than yourself how you should do it? You know the thing, you know your own mind best, and you have best the faculty of carrying it out. Besides, were you to ask counsel, those who give it would simply give such, very likely, as would suit their own ends, either their own honour, or their own gain. This temptation is much more dangerous and hurtful to persons that are devout and of good intelligence than to others, and it is indeed the height of pride.

8. Sometimes the devil has a trick of getting a man to speak things to his own dispraise, or even to commit sins, to show people that he is plainly not a hypocrite, and does not pretend to be over-good. Now this great evil is evidently suggested by the devil. For by this mode of speaking and acting

against his own glory, a still more subtle pride creeps in, since by acting in this fashion a man desires to be thought truthful and honest, and one who nowise seeks his own praise; whereas in his own mind this is the very thing he exceedingly burns with desire for. This is often very plainly to be discerned. For when some one else asserts the disgraceful things of the man, which he had said of himself, he shows himself very much annoyed, and takes up the cudgels in his own behalf, excusing himself hotly, and sounding the trumpet of his own praise in clear and loud notes.

9. The good of the neighbour is sometimes made a cloak for undertaking some noble and lofty enterprise. But the truth is, that our own ostentation and glorying hide beneath this cover. And this is plain, when he who would undertake it would rather the things were done by himself than by any

other person. For, if the thing could be done as well or even better by another, and that it would be just as pleasing to God that he should lose it as effect it, then to wish to do it shows evidently that self and his own glory is mixed up with the work. In fact, he would rather men knew the thing was effected through him than through others. It is a sign that the work is undertaken, not solely for God, but with an admixture of self. By this same touchstone the purity of our intention may be tested in other cases also.

10. Sometimes, under pretext of conforming to the ways and manners of others, and not being singular, or some other good and laudable virtue, the devil incites a person to eat and drink more than is fitting. So again of dress and other like things. Very great discretion must therefore be used in all things.

11. Sometimes a person holds

his tongue as it were from the virtue of silence when it is really from contempt, anger, or pride; and when he ought to speak, he does not, either through want of courage, or through human respect.

12. It happens also that under colour of a desire to know how to manage some necessary or useful thing, the enemy pushes a person to the hearing and seeing of many dangerous things, through curiosity and a craving to be acquainted with everything. Thence not unfrequently arise great temptations of unclean thoughts and images, or perhaps hatred. And even if nothing arise from thence, the thing itself is in a measure damaging to the soul. For the mind becomes so filled with the images of things seen and heard, that no peace or clear thought of God is possible. All is now obscured.

CHAPTER II.

Of Running into Opposite Extremes.

1. Our soul is sometimes full of sensible devotion, and this devotion may come from God, by a divine gift, and it may be stirred up by a simulation of the enemy of souls. Now in this heat of devotion, whether from God or from his own working, the enemy exhorts the soul to make indiscreet vows or rash oaths, that when the devotion is gone trouble may succeed at being thus involved, and perhaps the promises may be broken.

On the contrary, he at other times condemns all vows as indiscreet, and so he prevents a man from making holy vows against sins to which he is exceedingly prone, and by which he is vehemently tempted. This he does to sink him deeply and irretrievably in the mire.

2. The devil sometimes moves persons to chide others in passion, and so lose the fruit that might be expected. Some again he persuades to pass over in silence the defects and sins of others, which they are bound in charity to lay bare and reprehend, and he persuades them that it is a charitable mildness, whereas, really, it is the ruin of all virtue.

3. The souls of some are filled by the old enemy with countless scruples. He fills their consciences full of doubts and over-strictness. By this means he takes away their courage to do good works, and he causes that oftentimes they should sin. For though a thing be good, yet if by an erroneous conscience we judge it to be bad, and still do it, to us it is sin. The enemy

has another worse end to compass, namely, to get him who sins to fall into despair, judging himself to be reprobate, and to be a damned soul, seeing that he commits sin so often and so easily, and that he can in no way fulfil what he fancies that God commands him.

The devil acts just in the opposite way with others, getting them to sin freely with a secure and wide conscience, so that they neither fear to sin, and after having sinned they have no repentance.

A third method of the enemy is to make the conscience broad till the sin is committed, and afterwards to exaggerate the offence, showing its heinousness, and its enormity. Sometimes again he fills the conscience with fears where it has no right to fear. And in this he is like those who, when boys are passing along the road, cry out to them, "You'll fall, you'll fall," so that through their fear they may really stumble and fall. For to some the enemy cries out continually, "You are going wrong, you are committing sin, you are sure to be damned." Thus he disturbs the peace and quiet of the conscience, so that such can neither pray, nor set about any good work rightly. Now by this means he strongly urges often to commit sin boldly, so as to get rid of these scruples and fears by a large conscience: and this is a danger much more fatal and wicked, for thus an unbridled audacity is assumed, which cares for no precept, and judges nothing to be unlawful.

Now in all these temptations the middle pathway should be kept, wise and discreet persons should be consulted, recourse should be had to prayer, and above all things we should have a confidence in God mixed with a great humility, hoping in His sweet mercy.

4. Sometimes the devil infuses into the soul a most wonderful sweetness, having an appearance of devotion, that a man may rest altogether in this delicious enjoyment, not really loving God, and not rendering Him service, except only to get this delight by it.

But, again, at another time he will make the service of God hard and irksome exceedingly, filling the spirit with sadness, so that it shall seem that God has abandoned the soul. With this idea a man gives up his prayer, and turns to fleshly pleasures, to get from them some consolation. Thus those who love God with a love pure and unfeigned, and those who merely cleave to Him for their own pleasure, are proved and made known.

5. Some persons fancy they have a great spirit of prayer. So, instead of doing that work which is their duty, or fulfilling some other thing for those with whom they live,

leaving all other occupations, even those that are a duty, they wait upon God. Now this is a trick of the devil, that in this leisure he may the more easily fill the mind with unclean thoughts, or motions of rancour and anger, or temptations of vain glory, or the abominable itch of singularity.

The devil often makes a person value the good which is done of their own will, and which is in no way necessary, far higher than even a thing which is of obligation, and necessary to salvation. There are people who would rather break a fast of the Church, than one which they have set for themselves.

On the contrary, the devil urges some to continual active work, so that they may never be able to recollect themselves, or to make a faithful examen of their conscience. But moderation in both prayer and work is best, taking each by turns, so as to temper the one by the other.

6. On pretext of a zeal for truth, for justice, or public utility, the old enemy gets people to speak ill of their neighbour, and to do him a serious injury, their real motive being anger or spite. Sometimes the good or safety of others is made the plea, for the devil urges that a man's way of going on is likely to be dangerous to others, and his malice ought to be published, that they may be on their guard, and not to warn them would be against charity.

Now this fashion of dealing is highly risky, for those who are not the judges of others, and are not in the appointed position to punish them. Besides, to tell such like evils behind a person's back, to those who can in no way profit the person, or hinder the evils, what good can it do?

Now, on the opposite side, the

devil, sometimes by fears, through envy, or detraction, gets people to hold their tongues about a man's wicked ways, to his own ruin and the horrible destruction of the souls of others. The road then is full of snares, and it requires great discrimination to walk with safety, and escape the dangers.

7. The adversary of man sometimes offers to the mind pleasing fleshly thoughts, telling him that there is no danger in dwelling on them some little while, he has only to withhold all consent to any pleasure in them. Thus he gets a man to dally with the thoughts, and so burns and inflames his mind with them, that they stick to him like pitch, and he has hard to do to shake them off at last. There is no more wholesome plan therefore than to deny them all entrance at the very outset. Sometimes such hurtful thoughts arise from too close a study of the state of a per-

Snares of the Devil. 29

son's married relations, by one who is single.

On the other hand, the minds of some are so flooded by the enemy with vivid imaginations of unclean thoughts that they believe they are sinning continually. For these thoughts come in whilst they are saying their office, and praying to God. This, the enemy says, is horrible wickedness. He therefore exhorts them to give their attention to nothing else but this one thing, to root out completely these vile imaginations. The wicked one knows very well that one might just as well expect to be able to hold the wind in one's fist, as to have power to banish completely, root and branch, every foul imagination, without hope of return.

It is not a mortal sin when foul thoughts touch the mind, but only when we consent to embrace them with pleasure, and to rejoice in them, our will favouring them. When they displease us, and are hateful to us, and we have a horror of them, then there is no danger of mortal sin. We ought to know that in work time, and when doing business affairs, we cannot expect to have the same still serenity of mind as after a longish period of quiet. To seek for it is a vain labour, and only a temptation. These bad thoughts are often better put to flight by neglecting them, and giving no attention to them, than by battling against them. Occupy the mind with other things, and they will presently go of themselves.

8. It happens sometimes that the devil persuades a man to be too careful of his good fame, on the ground that to act otherwise would be to be cruelly savage towards himself. Now this over-carefulness leads to countless evils, for whenever such an one hears some fault has been imputed to him, he

straightway takes up the cudgels in his own defence, bringing forward excuses for his conduct, and praising all his actions, giving reasons for why he acts in this manner, and fancying by so doing to shut the mouths of men. Now this is impossible.

One who acts like this falls thereby into various evils, into anger, impatience, arrogance, and perturbation of mind. In order to maintain his own innocence he sometimes accuses others, or reveals things which it was his duty to keep strictly secret. By the same temptation he is led into hypocrisy and simulation, by imagining that others are ever occupied in scanning all his works. He does not wish to get the applause of the world; all his aim, he thinks, is to give good example, and secure himself from infamy. And he argues that when his good name stands unhurt, men will esteem his example more, and get more profit from his words. An opposite temptation to this is to hold cheap all that men may say or think of one. We are neither worse nor better for the opinion of men. So a man will say sometimes: A sin is just the same sin whether it be open or secret. By this people fall into a very careless way of living, and they justify themselves, saying, God knows my conscience, that is enough for me; let others say and think as they have a mind.

See, then, how hard it is to escape both snares, and so to walk on the right path as to be caught neither by the one nor by the other, for both are indeed most hurtful.

First, then, every one ought to consider what sort of a work it is he would do, good or bad. For if it be bad, by doing it openly he sins far more grievously. And in this case he is bound to hide it, not through pride, but to take from others an occasion of temptation, as also of evil speaking.

If the thing is good, but he knows that others, seeing it, may judge it to be evil, and that they would be brought so to judge from simplicity, or from not knowing the thing he does, or its motive; then, if the work is not necessary to salvation, it should be left undone for the time, or else its nature and goodness should be explained. Sometimes, however, a person's judgment of a thing comes from sheer malice; for there are some people that hate to see the virtue of another. There is nothing but what they try their tooth on. No attention is to be paid to these, for it is impossible to shut the mouths of such. There is no use in defending one's character against them.

Here it may be remarked that, as the Apostle teaches, God has been very often pleased to do sublime works by means of persons who were ignorant and of no parts, and who were in no esteem; more often indeed than by others. So a man ought not to wish that the good he does may be commended, and much less should he blow his own trumpet, and sound forth his own praise. All is to be left to God, who from nothing knows how to work great and marvellous things. Besides, we often see that the more careful a person is to make his innocence shine clear, or to bring his good into notice, the less is he esteemed or cared for by others. He profits himself far less, and others far less, in the ways of God.

CHAPTER III.

Of Good as a Handle to Evil.

Although good things are always good, yet they are made, by the craft of the devil, a handle to evil.

So he exhorts sometimes to high and difficult undertakings of virtue, such as immoderate fasts, very burdensome pilgrimages, and the like. He has various reasons. One is that a man may not be able to complete the thing promised; another, that by doing so some great damage may come to him, as for instance, that by excessive fasting he may injure his brain, may be filled with melancholy and oppressive sadness; or by the labours of a pilgrimage, that he may give way to vehement impatience; or from desire of being eminent in teaching others the swelling of pride may arise, or even the evil of heresy.

2. Sometimes, from an anxiety to give abundant alms, men are led by the devil to cheating, so as to get more money than is just or lawful. For he well knows that it is much worse to be dishonest in one's dealings in order to give largely,

than to give nothing, and utterly refuse all unjust gains.

3. Sometimes the enemy infuses into the soul a great sensible **sweetness** and moves her to tears, after going through a most severe and immoderate fast. He does this to encourage the person to continue indiscreet austerities, that thus the head may give way, and the brain be injured, and that afterwards melancholy or anger may ensue, and the body may be broken down. Or he wishes the person to give way to singular habits and to set him up by pride.

Sometimes the devil gives these tears and sensible sweetnesses after a very plentiful meal of meat and drink. And this he does to bring fasting and abstinence into disrepute, and to encourage a person to gluttonous living, as a means of procuring devotion.

4. The devil insinuates the vice of avarice, sometimes under colour

of a prudent care to provide security for declining years, sometimes the object is to lay up a sum for the poor, or for the building of a church. When the desire to get money is well established, he urges the soul, for a good end, not to be too strict in conscience, but to allow some fraud in buying and selling, or perhaps to swear falsely. No mortal sin is, however, allowable, however praiseworthy the end to be achieved may be.

5. The enemy has a trick also of hiding his working under the guise of devotion towards holy and religious persons, and a spiritual friendship; so that two persons, frequently talking, eating, and laughing together, may lose their guard, and take little liberties in joke, and that thus the holy and spiritual love may degenerate into an abominable carnal affection, and at last lead to a most shameful

6. When a man has begun to speak with a good and holy intention, the devil gets him to continue speaking; so that he may say words beside the purpose, and be moved by anger, or by vain-glory; or he gets him to think that the audience will think him dull if he does not tell them some news, or some extraordinary thing, or something ingenious. The end is that he talks in an unbridled manner, of what he knows and of what he does not know. Or, perhaps, he speaks of things that ought not to have been said before those persons, on account of their simplicity. The tongue, then, should be always curbed and measured, in the middle and end of our speaking, as well as at the beginning.

7. Sometimes the devil gives a man a fund of useful thoughts, but at the wrong time, and simply to hinder prayer. For he sends these thoughts for a bad end, and so at a

very unsuitable time. For when we are hearing or saying Mass, that is not a lawful time for planning on affairs of our household. At another time it would be very right and expedient.

8. It happens sometimes that a thought of anger or revengefulness shoots into the mind. Then this thought displeases the person, but the devil gives him to understand that it is evident he does not fully and freely forgive his enemy, therefore it would be wrong for him to say the Lord's prayer, or to receive the pax before communion. But if for God's sake a man wishes to love his enemy, he ought to, and he safely can, say to God: Forgive us our trespasses, as we forgive them that trespass against us. If with the will we love our enemy that is a true efficacious love.

9. Persons who fear God more than others, are tempted by the devil to fear Him more still, and to

be in continual terror in all they do. Such persons as these should get clearly and solidly instructed to what they are obliged by their state under pain of mortal sin, and what they are not obliged to. It is not possible to obtain an infallible knowledge on these points, but we may obtain a moral certainty, by the advice of prudent men, by the good counsel of devout persons, by the Scriptures, by the judgment of our own reason, by our confessor. Such a tempted person ought to conform his opinion to the judgment of these before mentioned. When, therefore, he has this kind of certitude, he may justly be in peace, even though he have committed some negligences or venial sins.

If, however, he becomes aware that he has failed in any principal points, then he ought to repent, and in fitting time and place confess. See, then, how necessary it is to be clear as to what is mortal sin, and what is not, what are obligations and what not. Then, whatever a person does over and above his obligations increases his merit and grace. But to believe that we are always bound to do what is best is an error, and to think that one who omits to do what he knows to be best, has, therefore, committed a mortal sin, is a foolish mistake. One who has these false fancies will never enjoy peace of conscience.

CHAPTER IV.

Of Curiosity in Various Ways.

1. Curiosity is made a snare of by the enemy of souls, and to some persons he gives a great craving to behold some miracle, or to have revelations. Then, either in sleep or when awake, he shows to such

certain deceitful appearances, to allure them to falsehood under the guise of truth, or to lift them up to pride. The devout soul ought therefore to flee such desires and detest them above all things. What others have experienced in these matters ought to be enough for us.

2. Sometimes the enemy pushes a man on to look into the sins of another, either to show them up and take away his good name, or that he may lose all love for him, and despise him, or that all wholesome counsel from his mouth may be rejected, or that all he does may be attributed to some bad intention. If the sins we observe are in our superior, he gives them as a reason why we should not be bound to obey him. If they are in a subject, they are esteemed a valid reason for most cruel treatment, and that such an one should be corrected without any mercy. Or again, the enemy tempts us to think that be-

cause we do not the like sins, we are therefore much better, and so he leads us perhaps into that pride which makes us really much worse. For this pride is a sin far more grievous than all the defects which, with such diligence and curiosity, we explore and consider in our neighbour.

We ought, then, to turn away our eyes from the looking on our neighbour's faults, and employ them in beholding our own. If we have the duty of examining or searching into the sins of others, it should be done with great compassion; for if we pity people for diseases of the body, how much more ought we to grieve for their diseases of the soul.

We ought also to pray God for them, considering that our own sins are still more grievous, or at least, had it not been for God's mercy, we should have been entangled in more heinous crimes. He who does not implore the divine mercy on the sins of others, as well as on his own, seems really guilty of hating his neighbour.

3. By curiosity, in searching into the wealth of our neighbour, the enemy of souls leads some into envy, trouble of mind, and melancholy. For by the sight of the pomp of riches, of carriages and horses, servants, fine clothing, &c., the mind becomes inflamed with covetousness, and a restless desire to be possessed of the same earthly glory.

4. A prying mind that would search too subtilly lays itself open to the most foolish and hurtful suspicions. The devil has a great hold of some souls by making them continually surmise that this or that thing was done for the very purpose of vexing them, or to make a mock of them, or to do them some injury. By these silly suspicions and misunderstandings temptations arise

Snares of the Devil. 45

between husband and wife, between brother and sister, between friend and friend. To suspect easily is a most fatal evil, for such suspicions, after having worked incredible mischief, are almost always discovered to be utterly groundless. They ought therefore never to be listened to. But if it is found impossible to get rid of them, it is a good plan that the one suspecting should ask of the other some satisfaction or explanation of the thing that causes the suspicion, so that there may be an opportunity of giving a reason that may dissipate all these doubtings.

But the devil takes good care often that the person he tempts shall keep the temptation quite a secret in his own heart. By this secrecy he prevents all hope of the clearing up of the circumstances that cause it, and he adds to it safely, as no opportunity of excuse or explanation is given.

However, sometimes he uses the very opposite method, and gets the person to blurt out his suspicions in a hot, rash manner, and most unseasonably. By this means a fierce tempest of anger is excited, which ends perhaps in the most malignant hatred. For the person feeling injured by the suspicion says to himself, "So this is the opinion that this man entertains of me, to suspect me so vilely without all reason. What have I done to merit it? Can he have a friend's feelings towards me who can so suspect?" The devil then makes his gains both ways, by silence and by speaking.

5. Some are tempted by the devil with a vehement longing to be present at the festival of a wedding, or other worldly vanities, and he so arranges that at the time, although they witness things and hear things not proper or modest, yet they feel in no way tempted

against chastity. This makes them very bold on this point, thinking they have reached a high degree of purity. Then by their presumption they give way to a proud elation, or they are emboldened to venture themselves more, and fall into immodest sins, or into very unclean thoughts. This does not always happen in the place, but perhaps afterwards, when they are alone, and when all they have seen and heard returns and fills their memory. It is safest, then, never to risk oneself needlessly, but to avoid the danger, and to put no trust in one's virtue.

6. The devil sometimes pushes a man to search into his predestination, to inquire whether God has destined him to glory, or foreknown that he will perish everlastingly. Then, if he thinks himself predestined to glory, he runs a danger of being lifted up by a presumptuous confidence; and if he think

the contrary, he goes headlong into a reckless despair. A man, then, ought not to form a judgment either way, but he should hope in the mercy of God, with a great fear of the strictness of His justice.

7. Sometimes a man is tempted to question within himself whether he would rather die, or would choose instead to be damned for ever; or again, whether he would be willing to commit a mortal sin rather than die. Now, if he choose rather to be damned, or to commit a mortal sin, rather than to die, he does by such a choice sin grievously, for we may not offend God to escape any misfortune whatsoever. But if he affirm that he would choose the other part, first, it may be a lie on his part, or self-deceit; then again, he may fall into a boastful arrogance, on account of the seeming firmness of his virtue. Such manner of questions, then, ought to be avoided. If they arise

in the mind, we should reject them without giving any answer to them. Instead of answering, we should say to God, "Thou knowest my frailty, O Lord; I confess that even a small pain would make me fall from Thee, were it not for the help of Thy grace. I cast myself therefore into Thy hands, beseeching of Thee never to let me be so tempted as to consent to transgress Thy commandments."

By this means we may safely pass over this perilous and malicious snare of the devil, that is, by acknowledging with lowly mind our own proper frailty, but putting all hope and trust in God, and by refusing to form any judgment on the matter. We know how S. Peter, when he had declared that he would rather die than deny our Lord, afterwards broke his promise, and forsook Him. Very many others act in the same way, thinking before they are tempted that they would be willing to suffer anything rather than sin, as though they could avoid sin by their own power only, without the help of God's grace.

8. Another temptation of a somewhat similar kind is this. When a person remembers some wickedness he did in his past life, by which nevertheless he enjoys some present good; as, for instance, by fornication or by adultery he has a child whom he loves intensely. Then comes the question to his mind, Would you rather have not sinned, and be deprived of this child, or have this child, consenting to the sin for it? Now, as in the former temptation, so here, whichever way he answers he runs the risk of being caught in a snare. The remedy, then, is not to answer the question. However, a man may grieve for the sin, and that by the sin he had a child, without grieving absolutely because he has a child.

9. There comes sometimes the question before the mind as to whether we be worse than other men, or than this or that man. From this source arise many sins, such as falsehood, pride, rash judgment. One so tempted should therefore reply, "Whatsoever proceeds from me, from my own fund, is sin; if there be in me any good it is of the grace of God, and God can equally give to any other what He gives to me. Now, when I have nothing of my own but sin, what use is there for me to compare myself with others, since I am of myself most wicked?"

10. The enemy places often before the eyes of the soul the graces and gifts that are in her, to puff her up, and make her despise others. Now, a person so tempted ought to consider that if he does not use the gifts of God well he incurs greater perils, and will receive a more intolerable damnation. Or he may

remember that there is no one, however wicked, who might not perhaps use the graces he has better than himself, so that he may not judge any one, Jew or Gentile, to be worse than himself, and all may be better.

11. A temptation not uncommon to repentant souls is to examine whether their contrition is such as God will accept of, and they argue that for some temporal misfortune they grieve and weep far more than for having offended God by sin. They consider, then, that their contrition is evidently not sufficient. But we should know that it is not necessary that we should feel so great a sensible sorrow for sin as perhaps we do for some earthly loss or misfortune. It is enough that the sin displeases us, and that we will never to offend God by the like sin any more. We are not obliged to wish rather to die, or to be damned, or to be stripped of all

our goods, than to sin, or than to sin in this or that manner.

Again, we are not obliged to have a sorrow answering to the divine immensity, which we have offended, for that were impossible. For the Godhead is infinite, but our sorrow at the very utmost can only be finite. The above-named sorrow, then, is enough.

It is true indeed that that sorrow is the best which is greatest in both soul and body, if only discretion is used in the sorrow of the body. For by bodily sorrow the health may give way, or the reason be injured.

Many temptations are avoided by the above mode of dealing, which are wont to arise when a person fears that he is never sorry enough, or that he has not done what he is bound to. He has done what he is bound to for salvation; but what we are bound to in consideration of the exalted nature of the Godhead, this we cannot do. We cannot repay Him the benefits He bestows. But our indulgent Father does not expect this of us. By His wondrous kindness it suffices to make us His friends, if only in certain number, and at certain times, we do the things He has commanded us under pain of eternal damnation.

Now all these precepts are contained in two, to love God above all things, and to love our neighbour as ourself. But if it be asked, what is signified by loving God above all things, I answer, plainly and simply, It is so to love Him as to love nothing else in such a way as to make you lose thereby the love of God. To love our neighbour as ourself is to wish eternal salvation for him, and grace in this present life, and also to do for him whatever in justice and reason we would wish him to do for us in the like case. For it is evident that one who is a judge ought not to will to set a robber free from gaol, though perhaps were he himself in prison he would wish, contrary to reason, to be set free. An answer may in like manner be given to various other temptations of this kind.

12. A penitent will sometimes inquire of himself whether he has now a firm purpose not to sin again. Then the devil proposes doubts to him, especially telling how frail he is, that he still falls often, and perhaps even daily. The penitent however ought to consider that it is perfectly true that he cannot through his own strength hope to escape sin. He ought not to say that he will never sin again, for to say so would be presumption; nor ought he to judge that he will sin, for this would be already to transgress. It is enough, then, to make a firm purpose, with the help of God, to avoid sin, and to use diligence to do so, and by one's present

will to give no consent to sin for the future.

13. When a person is going to communion the thought of his unworthiness comes sometimes into his mind, and a doubt whether he ought to approach; a doubt, too, perhaps, whether he has rightly confessed his sins, for he feels as if he had not made a real good confession. But such an one ought to consider that he never can by his own strength make himself worthy to approach the sacrament of the altar, no, not if he laboured to prepare himself for a hundred years. For this is required a divine gift, and God can give that at once just as easily as in a hundred years.

Again, he ought to consider that in this life no one can tell, with an infallible certitude, whether he be in a state of grace or not, whether he be truly penitent or not, whether he has made a good confession or not, unless God were to let him know by a special revelation. Therefore he who will not go to communion unless he has this certainty deceives himself, and seems guilty of a kind of pride.

There is, however, a moral certainty, which in our purpose is required, and which suffices. And this we have, when, in our recollection and examen of conscience, we find we have done that, which both our own discretion and the good counsel of others suggested, and have for some time been wont commonly so to do. But if our own judgment should not accuse us of mortal sin, then there is no new peril in going to holy communion, even though, as it may often happen, some slight doubts may come into our mind. These doubts we ought to repel, and we ought to force ourselves to act contrary to them. I call that a slight doubt, when a person judges of a thing, rather that it is just and good, than that it is evil; yet some reasons or thoughts occur to the mind, leading to some hesitation, but still the first judgment appears far the most certain. Now if both sides seem equally probable, we ought to stop till we get more ground for decision one side or other, either by the help of our own reason, or by consultation with others, or by a divine inspiration obtained through prayer. For unless in this mode a person obtain security in himself, he will always judge that he has made a bad confession, and will never feel easy or at peace, and this can never be good.

CHAPTER V.

Other Deceits of the Devil.

1. The devil does not always tempt a man unceasingly, but at certain times there is a lull. Then a man begins to think himself secure, and to neglect all precautions of defence, and the enemy rushes on him all of a sudden, when he is quite unprepared for the assault, and darts at him some fierce temptations of hatred, envy, lust, and the like.

This lull has, however, sometimes another object, namely, to cause pride. For, seeing that no temptation assaults him, a man is sometimes thereby lifted up, supposing that now he has vanquished all his enemies, and completely routed them, so that he has merited from God to be left in peace. Or again, he takes occasion therefrom to despise those who are still tossed with temptation.

2. The devil will often allow a man at peace to do many good works, provided only that in one point he sin deeply. If he has one free entrance into the castle of the soul, he thinks it enough, he is secure of its capture. This temptation, however, he often keeps concealed till death is coming. Then he is wont to fight more fiercely, and with more crafty cunning, knowing that, if he then fail, he will completely lose everything.

3. When any one hears another detracting some one, and dislikes the detraction, yet the devil often manages that through human respect he should confirm the evil that is said, or at least that he should be silent; for the devil knows that it is no small sin either to detract, or to hear patiently one's

neighbour thus lessened. For such an one ought to show how he dislikes the detraction, and this he may do, either by word, or by a grave countenance, or some other mode. He could say to the detractor that it would be much better to tell about his good deeds than his evil ones, or that it would be better to tell of his deeds to himself, so that he might amend, instead of speaking of them to another.

4. Dreams are made by the devil to some an occasion of great superstition, for by some an absolute credence is given to them, contrary to the precept of the Church of God, as if by dreams one could tell with certainty of future events. Other omens are in the same manner believed, as, for instance, that to meet a dog or a hare in the morning is the sure sign of an unlucky day.

Now the simple people are so full of manifold superstitions that it fills one with horror to even think of it. The devil puts these things into their minds to displease God, for he knows that men thereby confide, and put their trust rather in these things than in God. These superstitions are imprinted on their hearts, because they will not listen or give heed to the wise, and because they have such wicked minds that whatever happens they attribute it to some mad folly. For instance, if some good happens, they say at once, "I thought this would happen, for I saw such and such a thing in a dream." Nor do they thank God, attributing to Him, as the Author of all good, that which they have received, but with impious credulity they refer it to another source.

But as it often happens that some evil happened to them the same day, they say it happened because they saw something, or because a dog or a hare met them.

With the same folly they attribute a cure to some short form of words uttered, or some such like charm, not to God or nature. These things have no reason, and are strictly forbidden by holy Church. Far better to have recourse to God and to His Saints, and to trust in them, than in such mad follies. Let all thus beware of such melancholy fancies, and especially dissuade the young from having any confidence in them. For it is hard to root out of the mind what we have imbibed when we were young.

5. A good life has its difficulties, and is not always pleasant. The enemy sometimes fills the mind with sadness, and counsels to seek consolation in worldly delights. Two evils arise from this; the first, that not unfrequently people give way to foolish talking, and even draw others into sin; the second evil is, that the sadness of mind and disrelish of spiritual things be-

comes aggravated by this mode of treatment. For though a little worldly solace may have brought relief for the time, the spiritual sadness becomes worse than before. One, then, who would be rid of it must resist it stoutly; then it will depart, never to return.

6. Sometimes the enemy counsels a person to give way to some sin just for once, that being satisfied to the full, the desire of it may then cease, and there may be no more return to it. Now he does this, knowing, first, that a great sin will be thereby committed, and secondly, because, though a full satiety will take away the desire just for a time, yet the desire will afterwards return with increased force. When persons in a fever get a drink of cold water, they are for the moment greatly relieved, but afterwards the burning thirst is still more afflicting. So, when lust is satisfied, the desires are afterwards more vehement than

before. So again, those who have an itch find relief by scratching, but the diseased skin is made worse by their yielding, whereas, if only for a little while they overcome the desire, and endure their pain, by and by it ceases of itself, or at least it becomes tolerable.

7. It may, then, be taken as a general rule that as the good Angels turn all events, whether adverse or prosperous, whether good or evil, to the profit of the soul, to its salvation and perfection, so the devil, on the contrary, turns everything to its hurt. If any one abounds in riches, the enemy tries to make him abuse them, either by pride, by luxury, by usury, or by wrong acquisitions. Our good Angel, on the contrary, strives to make us thankful to God for them. He persuades us to give large alms, and to be content with the goods we have acquired. So in the consideration

of beauty, strength, knowledge, rank, high reputation, and their contraries, such as deformity, poverty, obscurity, our good Angel knows how to turn all to profit, and the devil knows how to turn all to our ill. For instance, the devil excites a person to enter Religion that afterwards he may leave it. But the good Angel endeavours that he may persevere in it and be constant. The devil tempts with pride and envy, but the good Angel encourages him to resist stoutly, and so merit more. By temptations a man is thus often benefited, so that the devil ceases sometimes to tempt, lest by vanquishing the temptation the goodness of a man should be augmented.

Against all the manifold temptions of the wicked one there is but one general remedy, as was revealed to S. Anthony, and that is humility, by which a man puts his whole trust in the help of God and of His Saints, attributing all his victories to the grace of God alone.

But though all is to be attributed to God's grace, a man must not on this account grow slack in rendering due service to God in the keeping of His commandments. For as we must attribute man's salvation to the mercy of God, so it must be borne in mind that by negligence man may render himself unworthy of this mercy.

Now, if the devil should say to a man, "Whatever you do, God knows already whether you will be saved or will be damned, and it cannot be altered;" let him answer, "Whatever God may have decreed concerning me, He is still always worthy to be loved and worshipped, nor can He prove false to those who serve Him; to those who do their best He will infallibly give the eternal glory of heaven. Although my own eternal lot is unknown to me, yet I know well that a good life leads to a good end, nor ought I, on account of this uncertainty, to fail in my duty to my God. Nay, as a sick man does all he can for his cure, though he knows not if his efforts shall succeed, so must I strive more and more for this great end."

In conclusion, it must be said that nothing instructs a man in the foregoing temptations and all others as the grace of God; and this grace is obtained by devout prayer, a deep humility, and heartfelt contrition. This grace, by the merits and intercessions of all the Saints, may the Father, Son, and Holy Spirit mercifully vouchsafe to us. Amen.

Contents.

	PAGE
Biographical Notice	3
Preface of the Author	9

CHAP.
I.—Of Vice under the semblance of Virtue	13
II.—Of Running into opposite Extremes ...	21
III.—Of Good as a handle to Evil ...	34
IV.—Of Curiosity in various ways ...	41
V.—Other Deceits of the Devil ...	59

www.ingramcontent.com/pod-product-compliance
Lightning Source LLC
Chambersburg PA
CBHW020254090426
42735CB00010B/1913

* 9 7 8 3 7 4 1 1 9 4 8 6 3 *